Wealthy IMMIGRANTS

How to Build, Grow and Preserve Your Wealth In Canada

Revised version

Jessica D. Pang

Published by Black Coral Publishing in BC, Canada
First version was published on Oct 18, 2013

Available from Amazon and other book stores
ISBN 978-0-9920864-3-5

I dedicate this book to the memory of my mother,
who always pushed me to achieve beyond
her expectations,
and to my wonderful children. They are the reason
I became who I am today.

I have come to realize that no experiences are
wasted in life, especially painful ones.

Acknowledgement

To MJ, who inspires me in so many ways, who encouraged me to surpass the limitations I set for myself, and to finish this project that was on my mind for almost 5 years.

Table of Contents

Introduction

The Land of Immigrants

"Canada is often referred to as a land of immigrants because millions of newcomers have settled here and helped to build and defend our way of life, starting with settlers from France and England." (Backgrounder — Facts in Canada's Immigration History).*

There is no doubt that Canada has become one of the best countries in the world in which to live. Immigrants from all over the world have helped to build this country during the last 146 years. According to Statistics Canada, *"In 2011, Canada had a foreign-born population of about 6,775,800 people. They represented 20.6% of the total population, the highest proportion among the G8 countries...More than 200 ethnic origins were reported in the 2011 National Household Survey (NHS). In 2011, 13 different ethnic origins had surpassed the 1 million mark."**

On Feb 27, 2013, Citizenship, Immigration and Multiculturalism Minister Jason Kenney said, *"Immigration is a key part of the government's plan to grow our economy, spur job creation, and ensure long-term prosperity for all Canadians."* At the same news release it was also said, "*Each year since 2006, Canada has admitted an average of about a quarter of a million immigrants.*"*

Times have changed. Over the last 15 to 20 years, many new immigrants have arrived already with a good education and work experience, and some were very successful before they came to Canada. From 2003 to 2012, about 43.48% of these permanent residents had a Bachelor's degree or higher education background; about 59.38% of these permanent residents belong to the 'economic immigrants' category. "*Economic immigrants are people selected for their skills and ability to contribute to Canada's economy, including skilled workers, business immigrants, provincial and territorial nominees, and live-in caregivers.*" (Facts and figures 2012 — immigration overview: permanent and temporary residents report from Citizenship and Immigration Canada).*

But one thing did not change. Just like the immigrants before them, they bring skills and knowledge to this new land along with their wealth. They all want to blend into Canadian society, contribute to it, and enjoy the opportunities and benefits this fine country has to offer.

There is something unique about this new group of immigrants. Most of us go through what I call the three-step emotional rollercoaster when we come to Canada. We build up our anticipation when we apply for immigration, we land in Canada in our expensive clothes, buzzing with excitement, and we start our new life with fear after spending half or more of our life savings in a few months, trying to settle in. Then, we realize it is a very different culture and system, and we need to learn how to swim in this water. Even if you were a well-educated and skilled professional or a successful business owner in your old country, this is a new beginning. You have a very good foundation to start, but how do you make your new life in Canada another success?

When I first came to Canada, I made a lot of painful mistakes as an immigrant. Not only did these mistakes cost me a lot of time and money, I was also extremely frustrated. Before moving to Canada I had a successful career. After I came here it took me several years to understand the system well enough to finally reach some of my goals: goals that I initially thought would be easy to achieve. This is why I chose to share these financial planning methods with other Canadian immigrants, to help you achieve the level of success you deserve in a much shorter period of time. This book is not only for the foreign-born immigrants. It is for all Canadian residents who are hungry for information on managing their finances in Canada, no matter if you are a first-, second- or even third-generation immigrant.

Drawing on my financial planning background, together with my work experience in administration, marketing and banking, I will provide you with some tools to become a financially-empowered immigrant. You will learn some techniques to make the most of financial opportunities. With this knowledge, you will have the potential to make timely and solid financial decisions that support your lifestyle, and turn them into prosperity in Canada. We all have stories of personal struggles that have landed us in our own life situations, and I am here to assist you in developing a personal life plan of your own. I hope this book will introduce you to a road map to change your personal story of struggles into a more positive outcome. You will make less detours when you are on your way to achieving your ultimate success — your happiness.

* Citizenship and Immigration Canada website
  Statistics Canada website

To your happiness and prosperity!
Jessica Danli Pang

State of Mind

What Does it Has to Do with My Financial Success?

Dictionary Definitions of 'State'—[steyt], *noun, adjective, verb,* **stat·ed, stat·ing.** *

The condition of a person or thing, as with respect to circumstances or attributes: *a state of health.*

The condition of matter with respect to structure, form, phase, or the like: *water in a gaseous state.*

Status, rank, or position in life; station: *He dresses in a manner befitting his state.*

The style of living befitting a person of wealth and high rank: *to travel in state.*

A particular condition of mind or feeling: *to be in an excited state.*

An abnormally tense, nervous, or perturbed condition: *He's been in a state since hearing about his brother's death.*

A politically unified people occupying a definite territory; nation.

The territory, or one of the territories, of a government.

13

Are You in the Right State of Mind To Be a Successful Immigrant in Canada?

You are most likely thinking, "What are you talking about? Are you going to tell us all the tricks of financial planning in Canada? Don't waste our time. Get to the point!" Yes, I will do that shortly. First at all, take a deep breath and ask yourself, "What do I want from this change? Why did I come to Canada? Do I have a plan for my future?"

I hear you laughing. This woman is crazy, she wants to give us a philosophy lesson, and we do not even know what tomorrow will bring us. You can laugh, but just bear with me. No matter why you have come to Canada, how much you have or do not have right now, and where you want to go with your life, **I believe we all want the same thing: a better quality of life. You will not get to where you want to be unless you know the exact destination and how to get there.**

Do These Stories Sound Familiar to You?

A Chinese businesswoman argues that she is usually extremely lucky, and always ends up at where she wants to be. But how often does that happen? Is she just lucky? Her husband, a new immigrant like her, is the complete opposite. He wastes too much time without direction instead of getting to where he needs to be! Many of us are somewhere in between. As a new immigrant, you may start to feel lost; you might even become frustrated. Very often you will start to lose patience and hope.

Then you may tell yourself that there is no way you can reach your goal. Maybe it is not meant to happen; maybe there is a better place for you other than Canada. So you start to give up; and you tell yourself that next time you will succeed. Or you lie to yourself that you don't care about that loss, and you don't need to prove yourself to anyone!

These failure stories often build momentum and continually repeat themselves. Finally, your energy is drained and your precious time is wasted. Ultimately, you are left feeling depressed and you feel like you're a loser; that you failed to build a new life in Canada; that it's too hard. You do not have the support system to get you there. You then either decide to go back to your own country or stay and just feel miserable.

Unfortunately, that is the life story of so many immigrants after they move to Canada. Do you want yours to be the same, or do you want to follow a different life path? You can have a completely different story if you learn from others' mistakes. **That is why you first need to embrace a new state of mind before you even listen to my advice on financial planning.**

I came to Canada because I wanted an MBA from McGill University. I had a good solid foundation in education and work experience back in China and Hong Kong. I planned to get an MBA in Canada and then return to Asia. When I found out I needed to pay much higher tuition fees than local students, I decided to apply for Canadian immigrant status instead of being an international student. I even studied French for a year to prepare for my immigration interview.

I landed in 1997 in Vancouver and flew to Montreal right away. I left my past behind and arrived with two suitcases and a backpack. I also brought enough savings for me to live on for a few years without having to work. You might think I had less fear than some other immigrants, but that is not true.

I have been through all the ups and downs all immigrants have been through. I have witnessed other immigrants go through the same cycles repeatedly, from high and happy to low and depressed, and back again. I have first-hand experience with the ugly stories of surviving as a new immigrant in Canada. Finally, I got to the point in life where I stood on my own two feet and had proudly blended into Canadian society. I am now calm and content. I am confident I can do more, and know that better is yet to come.

Embracing a New State of Mind is the Beginning of Your New Success

Do you have a clear vision of what you want to achieve? Who do you want to become? Where do you want to go? When do you want that to happen? Most importantly, why do you want these? If you do not know what I am talking about, then you really need to continue reading.

If you have been through some extreme difficulty in your life, you will understand what 'in a dark place' really means. I was in that place during the spring of 2012. I decided to go to an Anthony Robbins 'Unleash the Power Within' seminar in New York.

While it was costly for the whole trip, I went anyway. Although I was afraid of that famous fire-walk process like everyone else, I went through it without being burned. That was the time I truly understood that fear is just fear. How I condition my mind can make a significant difference to my being. I witnessed many life-changing moments during those 3 days. I realized the biggest mistake I made in life was not having a clear vision. I failed before I even started. The blueprint of my life was made under the influence of my parents and society. I finally made a decision to change my old patterns. My health issue disappeared magically at the first night of that seminar. I started to see the whole picture of my life and I now have a new blueprint for myself that is exactly what I want from my life.

I spent time learning the systems from those who had already succeeded in the areas I wanted to excel in, and found a method that works for me. The process is like creating the ideal car for yourself. You have a list of features you want for your dream car, and you think you need to build it from scratch. Imagine how long it takes to get the kind of engine you want, the special tires, the shape of the car and the colour...the list goes on. But wait, what if this car is already available? You can just shop around and choose the model you like. Customize with a few small changes if it is really necessary. Enjoy the great work of the experts in car design instead of inventing the whole car!

Find Your True Passion and Your Own Drive

Ask yourself: What makes you happy? I mean, really happy? Find things you will have interest in for a very long time, things you don't get paid to do but will do anyway, and that really are your true passion. You may be surprised. The value you will get from your passion could represent much more than just money.

In my opinion, being able to take control of one's life path is one of the best qualities in humans. That is why some people are described as energetic and vibrant. Because they know the purpose of their life, they are more self-motivated and courageous. No matter what stage of life you are at right now, you can benefit from finding your own driving force.

When you are driven, it will give you self-motivation. Self-motivation will bring out the energy and talents in you. Ride on that energy and use all your talents, it will reward you with fulfilment. Fulfilment is a measure of the quality of life. If you are content, you are able to bring happiness to others as well. That is when you reach your ultimate goal of success. Your life now has more depth.

Blueprint of Your Own

Many of us have a goal to pursue, often because society or our parents encourage us to set one. After you reach your goals for other people, you have to face the truth. Now what? I am here, but I am not happy, because I am not being myself, I am not being understood and heard. It is extremely important to know that your blueprint in life should be developed from your innermost desires and wants, not from those of your parents or society. Once you identify what you really want, you can draft your blueprint yourself. In Canada, you will find the culture is different, and you will have more personal space for everything. You will experience more freedom to express your true being and mind. If you think outside the box, you will eventually find a way to keep the best of your own culture while learning from the culture of the best country on earth.

I hope by now you know what you want from this new immigration experience. You have set your state of mind for success, you have found your true passion and you are ready to do much more than just survive. Now you are ready to have a self-fulfilling and rewarding experience while blending into Canadian culture and adopting Canadian standards. Are you ready to be responsible to yourself, your family and Canadian society and have success in this new land?

*dictionary.reference.com

CHAPTER 2

Financial Planning

We Buy Houses, Gold and Own Term Deposits

Three True Stories

My mother was an accountant who had a successful career before she came to Canada. When I told her that many Canadians like to keep their valuables in a safety deposit box she laughed. *"You cannot find a place to hide your valuables in such a big house? Who needs to pay for a safety deposit box at a bank?"*

During her stay with us, she organized my house. Eight years later, I sold my house. The house inspector found some paintings wrapped in plastic, hidden in the attic. They were original papaya paintings from Egypt. I wondered for a long time how they had magically disappeared. So I asked my mom what else she had hidden for me, but she could not remember. I still wonder about some of my precious items, such as the set of rare metal stamps I collected for years. They might still be stuck somewhere underneath the drawers of the furniture I donated to the Salvation Army. Or maybe they are still at a 'safe corner' in my old house.

The inspector also joked, *"I bet you did not keep a record of those important items. Otherwise you could claim them through your house insurance policy."* Later I confirmed that was true, the coverage was built into my house insurance policy. I had already paid for it. All of these items were lost and I could not recover the value because we were still dealing with things as though we were back home in China.

———————&—————————

Three young men immigrated to Canada and they were ambitious to build a good life here. That is the reason most people move to Canada in the first place. They gathered all their savings and opened a computer store. But they did not want to spend money on insurance. They wondered how often they would need to claim on it. They had never heard of anyone doing that before in their old country and it seemed fine. However, thieves broke into their store after the grand opening and took all the valuables. These three tough looking men broke down in tears. They did not even have money for food because they used it all to cover expenses after the burglary. Their friends finally knew the truth and brought food for them.

———————&—————————

An experienced businessman from China bought a farm after he immigrated to Canada. He focused on producing a new kind of mushroom that was not on the Canadian market. The future looked very bright for his business. Again, insurance was not something in his business plan. Although he knew the farm building was too old and no insurance company wanted to insure it, he decided to take the risk and continued using it. One hot summer day, a fire caused by the high temperature burned the entire farmhouse to the ground. You could see smoke from miles away. Thankfully no one was hurt.

These stories broke my heart. I understood the thinking of these entrepreneurs as we came from the same background. I felt their pain as I was also a new immigrant and business owner. Although they both rebuilt their businesses from scratch, the outcome could have been very different if someone had provided proper professional advice to them, and they had actually taken that advice to avoid these costly mistakes.

Why Do I Need Financial Planning Advice?

Those who came from Mainland China, Taiwan and Hong Kong have found a big difference in financial systems and services between Asia and Canada. The first thing they discover is that they have to pay fees to the banks to keep their money. That sounds like a joke to them. I researched financial services before landing in Canada. I also used to work at banks in Hong Kong and China. I thought I was clever enough to handle my own financial affairs. I opened all kinds of accounts the second day after I got off the plane. Soon after, the stock market dropped steeply. I never received a letter or call from my account manager to explain the market situation. Even when I went to the branch, my account manager did not give me any advice. I sold my mutual funds at a loss. My account manager also never mentioned the taxation consequences. Many years later I took an income tax preparation course at H&R Block. Then I understood that she may not even have had adequate training and knowledge to provide me with the proper advice. It could also have been that her company policy was restricted her providing such advice to me.

The taxation system is complicated in Canada. The investment products are different. New immigrants absolutely need professionals who have lots of knowledge to help them. The ways from the old country might not exactly work in Canada. **In order to make your life much easier and succeed in Canada, you want to have at least three professionals on your team: an accountant, a financial planner and a lawyer. Their jobs are not in conflict with each other. Together, you have a team to analyze your past, plan for your future, and fix your issues when challenges arise.**

Do You Need a Financial Planner? Ask Yourself These Questions:

1. Do you want to spend time on all the research necessary to make an investment decision, or would you rather spend that time on other important things?

2. Do you know how to **reduce your bad debts**?

3. Are you strong enough not to follow the behaviour of others, such as spending habits or impulsive investment decisions?

4. Do you have a budget that considers all the implications?

5. Do you know how much you should set aside for short-term resources?

6. Do you have a plan if you cannot work for a few months because of sickness or disability, and know how it will impact your retirement savings?

7. Do you have strategies for saving for future large purchases, such as a house, car, cottage, boat, or any other big event such as a wedding?

8. Do you know how to make your **mortgage interest tax deductible**?

9. Have you set up **different tax-advantaged plans** that could ensure your kids have enough saved for their **post-secondary education**?

10. Do you have a written retirement plan to help ensure you have enough money in retirement?

11. Are you disciplined enough to stay focused on your long-term plan?

12. Do you know how to invest in a tax-efficient way?

13. Do you understand current market events and how they may impact on your investments?

14. Do you know the **strategies of income split** with your spouse and other family members within the guidelines of Income Attribution rules from the Canada Revenue Agency (CRA)?

15. Do you know what rebalance means and what it does for you?

16. Are you planning to start a small business or sell your business soon?

17. Do you have a **business succession strategy**?

18. What should you do when the market is higher or lower?

19. Do you remember to change your financial plan when different life events happen such as relationships, children, job, education, or health issues?

20. Do you know where to find a trusted expert such as a lawyer, a tax planner or an accountant when you need one quickly?

21. Do you know how much is **enough for an early retirement**?

22. Do you know what legal **tax shelters** there are for your investments?

23. Do you have an **estate plan**? Or do you have anyone who will walk you through the process after the passing of a loved one?

24. Do you know how much money you need to support you over your lifetime?

25. Do you know which income stream you should use first to get the **maximum taxation benefit during your retirement**?

26. Do you know how to plan for tax-efficient retirement income?

27. Do you know if your investment is safe and how to protect yourself from fraud?

28. Do you know the strategy to **protect your children's inheritance** from the potential chance of separation or divorce in the future?

29. Do you know how to **transfer your assets to the next generation, and how to do this tax free**?

30. Do you want to leave a legacy long after you are gone?

From this extensive list, you get the picture of what a financial planner could do for you. The role of a financial planner is different from an accountant. A good financial planner is much more than just an investment advisor, or insurance agent, or Registered Education Saving Plan (RESP) sales representative...

What Exactly is Financial Planning?

Financial planning might be a new concept for you. According to Wikipedia, "*A financial plan is a series of steps or goals used by an individual or business, the progressive and cumulative attainment of which are designed to accomplish a final financial goal or set of circumstances. e.g. elimination of debt, retirement preparedness, etc.*"

In a simple sentence: Financial Planning is about planning to achieve your financial goals. It helps you to be a financially responsible person. One of my clients told me, "*What you did for me is not only a financial plan. This is life planning.*" It is true. It relates to the daily life of almost everyone. It is a life skill; it involves so much more than just money. The younger you have this life skill, the earlier you will succeed in life. Many parents have agreed with me that teaching children and teenagers to be financially responsible should be part of the high school education program.

My friend MJ suggested to me a simple strategy to teach children about managing their finance, with a little lemonade stand in the summer. From thinking of the details of when and where to put the stand, the children learn about a business plan. From managing cost and price, they learn about budgeting. From promoting and selling, they learn about sales skills and marketing method. From the whole process and the end result, they can learn the basic elements of a financial statement. What a brilliant idea! What it teaches is the spirit of entrepreneurship and the life skill to be financial independent.

You might see different definitions of Financial Planning; there are 6 components of Financial Planning, according to the Financial Planning Standards Council of Canada. They are:

- Financial Management;
- Asset Management;
- Risk Management;
- Tax Planning;
- Retirement Planning; and
- Estate Planning

Most people understand this definition as cash management or money management, investment planning, insurance planning, taxation planning, retirement planning and estate planning. Some people also consider education planning as a financial planning subject.

Financial planning has 6 basic steps:

1) Establish client-planner engagement
2) Establish objectives and gather data
3) Clarify present status and identify problems
4) Identify appropriate strategies and present plan
5) Implement the plan
6) Monitor and update

Financial Planning is a Lifetime Process

There are many stages in your life where you need help with financial planning. You might start a new job or a new business; you might be in a new relationship; you are raising young children or planning for your retirement. If you are already retired, you might want to know how long your savings will last and how much your income stream will be every year, and you may plan to pass your estate onto your next generation if you have more than you could use. A financial planner can be with you all the way. Then there are those unexpected events, such as: your relationship breaks down; you lose your job, become critically ill, have an accident, receive an inheritance, or even win the lottery. All these events are within the circle of wealth.

If you search the phrase 'circle of wealth' or 'wealthy circle', you will get lots of information. Although there are different opinions about the 'circle of wealth', I would like to summarize it into 3 major phases, each phase based not on age, but on wealth. It is very important to understand this concept, because I assume you do not want to have net debt instead of net worth in your 50s, or you cannot afford for food and medication in your 70s.

Phase one: Wealth accumulation. During this phase, you are building your wealth, and often spending heavily on raising young children. Those who are not disciplined enough on their spending will face significant consequences in the future. I will explain why in another chapter. To be very clear, I am not suggesting you should feed your family cat food to save money. But I am not a fan of living a lavish life style before becoming financially responsible.

Phase two: You have a net worth and enjoy your lifestyle. In this phase your total net worth is more than your total debt. Your mortgage is probably paid off, and other expenses are less than before. You are able to enjoy the lifestyle you want. You are at the peak of your income-earning years. You can save and invest much more than before. This is the time you really need to start your retirement planning. Some people confuse this phase with the first one. They spend so much as if they are in the second phase; in reality they are still in the first phase to build their wealth. In that case, they are building themselves a huge debt. But what if something happens and the high income stream does not come or does not last? What if the inheritance never comes because their parents need it all? Or that their parents even need financial support from them?

Phase three: Preserve and transfer your wealth. Usually in this phase, you retire from working and you withdrawal from your saving and investment. The earlier you retire, the longer you need money to support yourself. With medical technology improving so quickly these days, more and more Canadians are able to live to age 90 and beyond. Think about the inflation in 40 years. Are you ready to retire at 50? Do you believe the government will continue to have all the social programs, and for how much longer? For those who do well financially before retirement, you even have enough to transfer to the next generation or to charity.

During different periods of your life cycle, you will have different needs and focuses, not to mention those events you do not expect. A well-thought financial plan will help you through your path with ease.

You can see clearly now how financial planning is an ongoing process of a lifetime. Your financial planner can become one of your lifelong friends, especially when immigrants are new to Canada and need to adjust to many changes. Find professionals to join your team who will plan with you, help you settle in as smoothly as possible, and help you reach your short-term and long-term goals quicker and more easily.

C H A P T E R   3

Peace Paper

Talk to Me About it After I am 65 ...

I know this is not a subject some immigrants want to discuss, because very often they come from a culture that considers talking about death as bad luck. But we will all eventually leave this world even if we never talk about it. If you do not have your estate plan set up, it could cause HUGE issues in the future. Cantonese people call a will a 'peace paper'; such a paper gives you peace of mind. It is very well named.

Not Having a Proper Will

How many of you have heard those ugly stories of relatives fighting over an inheritance? It does not only happen to celebrities or millionaires. It happens more often than we care to hear. At the very least it creates tension between family members and in some situations it totally destroys relationships. Interpersonal dynamics can continue to affect you mentally and physically long after the battle is over.

For those who have failed to safe proof their wills against future family disagreements, their money may not be distributed as they intended. In one case, 10 siblings fought over a $50,000 inheritance after their father died. In another case, the majority of assets of a man who did not leave a will went to his newlywed young spouse instead of his own children from his previous marriage, and his widow had no intention of sharing those assets.

The worst case I know of involved a man who destroyed the last will of his mother, which was to benefit his sister the most. The mother put her son's name on her safety deposit box account because he lived in the same city. This man opened the safety deposit box without telling his sister before their mother passed away, and he destroyed that will. Later, when the truth came out, he told his sister shamelessly, that if he did not show her their mother's will—the one he destroyed--it meant the older will that would benefit himself was the only will. He did not care if he broke the law, nor was he thinking about their mother's wish and the reason behind their mother's actions.

Sadly, all of those mentioned either trusted the wrong person or did not think their estate planning through. Money is all that matters to some people. Fairness, honesty and compassion are not in their dictionary. I doubt all these terrible results were the intention and wishes of the parents. They would likely come out from their graves to fix it if they could.

The outcomes could have been completely different if these people had taken some time to have a proper estate plan done.

Reasons People Don't Think About Having a Will

What is the rush? Nobody is sick here!

This is what my mom said to me in our very last conversation before she passed away. I was planning to take her and my children for a vacation together. She said that no one was sick and what was the rush to see each other. One month later, she died suddenly. No one expected she would die so young. She was doing everything right. She never even discussed what she preferred for her funeral because she thought it was very unlucky to discuss such things, and she did not imagine herself dying unexpectedly.

I do not have many assets, and I have no family, why bother?

People who do not have many savings or any family at the moment often do not bother with a will, but it does not mean they will not have assets or dependents in the near future. The assets could come from an inheritance, a well-paid job or even the lottery. Who knows? You could name a charity as your beneficiary if you do not have any family now. At least you will help those in need. Dying without a will could mean that the vast majority of your assets go to the government. The most important thing is that your ability to make a will could be changed within seconds. It could be too late when you realize you need a will. I am not promoting fear here; I am being realistic and thoughtful. We should always have a Plan B to fall back on and then back to focus on building a bright future.

I have COMPLETE faith that bad things do not happen to me.

Are you laughing? There are people who really think this way. No matter which culture or religion you come from, there was only one person I have heard of who actually conquered death. Many emperors and kings from different countries tried to live longer than their life expectancy, but no one seems to have succeeded, according to history.

I have enough money to leave for my family, so they will not fight

Just look at the stories at the beginning of this chapter. I am NOT saying these battles will happen in all families, but the reality is some people will fight for any amount of money. **The larger the estate is, the bigger the fight could be, and the longer it would take to settle**.

It will cost me to have a lawyer draft a will.

If you die without a will, you will lose the chance to appoint the one you trust to be your executor. Usually it costs more to have an administrator appointed by a court to administer your estate. To save a few hundred dollars on drafting a will, you may lose much more in the future. When there is a valid will, your executor can act immediately after your death. But if you do not have a will nothing will be done until a court appoints an administrator.

If you die without a will, someone has to apply to the court and your entire estate will be subject to probate fees, including items like jewellery, family heirlooms, and collections you wish to pass onto family members or friends as gifts. The probate fee is different from province to province in Canada. **The process of probate is likely to be costly and time consuming.** A lawyer friend told me, *"Lawyers love will kits because you can easily miss important things when preparing the will yourself."* Will validation is so complex in Canada, I can see you running to the first lawyer you can find, and getting them to fix the mess for you. That can cost you thousands more dollars easily. **The worst case scenario is that your estate may go to the Crown.**

I am married/I am in a common-law relationship, my other half will get everything automatically if I die.

This is a huge misunderstanding. Not everything will go to the surviving spouse automatically. A common-law partner may not even benefit from your estate if you do not have a will.

How about blended families?

For blended families, the case is much more complicated. Having an updated will is absolutely recommended. Otherwise some people you wish to give to, like children from your previous relationship, may not receive your inheritance. **The law favours the current spouse. Be aware that the separated spouse still has a right of inheritance.** These laws may not reflect your preferences if you do not have an updated will.

A will — a 'must have' for parents with children

Having a will is extremely important for parents with young children. Firstly, if you pass away without a will, you basically lose the chance to choose the right guardian(s) for your children. Even if your relatives or friends wish to take care of your children, they still have to apply to court for guardianship. What if none of them are prepared for this commitment and the cost? What kind of family could these children be sent to? How are they going to be raised?

Choosing the right executor(s) and guardian(s) is not easy. It is recommended to choose different people to act as guardian and trustee. Ask their permission first before you put their name down. Depending on the size of your estate and your family situation, choosing two people to act as executor is better than choosing one.

Secondly, unless the court grants access, without a will your estate assets will normally be frozen. They are typically given to your children when they reach the age of 18 or 19, depending on the province of their residency. But how many parents actually agree that young adults will be mature enough to handle a lump sum of money wisely? By having a properly drafted will, the parents would have a chance to find the right person to handle the assets on behalf of their children.

Thirdly, you can indicate in your will when you want these assets to be given to your children. You could choose to give them a percentage at the time they finish university, for example. Of course, this involves an estate lawyer to set up a testamentary trust through your will, but the benefit of setting up this trust is much bigger compared to the cost. Also, there is a potential taxation benefit from this kind of trust, and the potential to prevent your children from being the target of a 'convenient' relationship. This is particularly important for the new immigrants who do not know much about Canadian family and estate laws.

Ask yourself these questions:

Am I a responsible parent? Am I doing my best to protect my children and raise them in the right way? Should I have a plan for them in case I die before they become adults?

Please DO NOT give away your very last chance to show them your love.

Solution: Have a Properly Drafted Tax-Planned Will

I suggest to all my clients that they should have an updated and properly drafted will, because it is part of the financial planning process. The biggest bill most Canadians ever pay in their life is the last tax bill. So having a properly drafted and tax-planned will means you have thought over many details of your life. There are strategies to help you save tax on your estate.

'Estate taxes' do not formally exist in Canada. It is a term many of us pick up from American shows profiling dramatic battles among family members over an inheritance. There are two very important Canadian taxes you should be aware of when doing your estate planning.

Income Tax Due to Deemed Disposition

In Canada, you cannot escape taxes even upon death. Instead, your estate administrators will be required to file taxes for your final year up until the time of your death. This can result in a whopping tax bill, which should be considered when you plan your will. Your final tax return (some call it 'terminal return') filing will include tax on:

- Income earned until the time of your death, from the time of your last tax filing that has not previously been taxed.

- Capital property owned at the time of death.

The capital property tax is calculated by treating all capital properties as if it was sold at the time of death at its fair market value (FMV). These capital properties do not just mean the real estate properties. The tax owing is then based on the capital gains and losses from the sale.

Similarly, tax is owed on any retirement investment vehicles—RRSPs (Registered Retirement Saving Plans) and RRIFs (Registered Retirement Income Plans)—at the time of death. These investments are considered sold at the time of death.

The good news is there are rollover provisions for certain situations to defer income tax, but there are also stipulations on how it is to be managed by the beneficiaries in order to retain the tax deferred status. You need a professional who can explain the rules and the best estate tax planning options for your particular needs.

Provincial Probate Fee

Upon death, wills are filed in probate court. A probate judge then ensures the estate assets are administered as planned by the deceased. The probate court charges a probate fee based on a percentage of the assets listed in the will. If a wealthy person leaves a $10 million estate, it will take the court more time to administer and allocate the assets. And, of course, the larger the amount of the estate, the higher the risk of a family battle over the estate assets. Although most wills are dealt with in a timely and efficient manner, some wills are tied up in probate court for many years. Probate fees vary from province to province in Canada.

Assets in USA

If you are one of the many Canadians with assets in the United States, you may still end up paying actual U.S. estate taxes. Paying taxes on foreign property can be a complex process due to multijurisdictional issues.

As I mentioned in the previous chapter, you need to have 3 professionals in your corner: an accountant, a financial planner and a lawyer. In this kind of situation, you will see the power of a team that works together for your best interest. By talking to an expert in the field, your estate can benefit hugely from professional advice. After all, it is your hard-earned money. Don't you wish to use it for the people you love and care about? Or leave it to the charity that is in your heart?

Store Your Will

Taking the time to draw up a properly prepared will is so important, as well as choosing the right executor(s) and guardian(s). Finally, remember to store the updated will in a proper place. **Remember to make duplicate copies of your estate documents, and keep them in different locations that you know are absolutely secure but still easy to find by your family**. Hint: The safety deposit box in the bank is not the best place to lock your Power of Attorney and living wills such as Representation Agreement for health care. I do not suggest you put anyone's name on your safe deposit account unless they are the one receiving your estate.

Last but not least, registered wills are public records in Canada. For those who wish to keep their life private, there are investment products that allow the asset to go to the named beneficiaries without the whole world knowing who is mentioned in your will.

Family and Estate Laws Are Not Exactly the Same from Province to Province in Canada

For example, if you live in British Columbia and you do not have a will, the default of estate law is: If you have a spouse and a child, the first $65,000 of your total estate assets goes to the legal spouse and the rest of the balance is split equally between the spouse and the child; if you have a spouse plus children, the first $65,000 of your total estate assets goes to the legal spouse, then one-third of the balance of your estate assets(your total estate less the first $65,000) goes to the legal spouse again, and two-thirds of that balance going to the children.* **With the recent changes made to family law in British Columbia in March 2013, and the new Wills Estates & Succession Act (WESA) is coming into force in March 2014, you absolutely should talk to your lawyer to understand how that has already affected or will affect you.**

A financial planner does not prepare wills for clients. You are strongly recommended to seek legal advice from a lawyer who practices in the province of your residence and the province in which your will is prepared. If you move to another province, it is best to have a review of your will by a lawyer in your new location.

* CCH Canadian Estate Planning Guide (November 2006)

CHAPTER 4

Risk Management
We Moved Here Because We Thought It Was a Safe Country

If you were raised to believe that fate and luck determined your experiences in life, risk management embraces the exact opposite view. In my opinion, luck is the combination of proper planning and an amount of preparation. With risk management tools, you can recover your losses in case your initial plans fail. You reduce the overall chances of failure, and change your fate for the better. Risk management strategies can help you protect and grow your wealth.

The sellers of tulips in the Dutch flower markets in the 17th century were probably among the first to use risk management tools to change their fate. Unlike many of us today, the Dutch tulip sellers were living the high life. Some tulips sold for 10 times the annual salary of a skilled craftsman. But some sellers knew this kind of market was temporary. When the tulip mania bubble burst, many tulip growers and sellers lost everything. To protect their income, the smarter tulip sellers developed risk management contracts to insure themselves against losses in the future. They paid a small upfront fee to guarantee the price of tulips at a future date (Wikipedia). By doing so, they changed their fate by securing their long-term income and transferred their potential losses to others.

Let's face it: we do not know our fate. Whether you talk about it or not, things happen and you cannot stop them.

The best thing is to be responsible to yourself and your family. You work hard for a good life. You need a Plan B in case things do not go the way you want. Many financial planners consider that risk management is the foundation of financial planning. Because no matter how great a job your financial planner does, the well-written financial plan will fail if you do not have continued income, or even worse if you die and leave your family behind without financial support.

Risk Management Is Not Just About Insurance

Risk management is not all about insurance products. First at all, you will need an Insurance Needs Analysis to determine if you need extra insurance coverage. Everyone's situation is unique. From the result of the Insurance Needs Analysis, you will know right away if you have enough resources to cover your risk. If not, then there are insurance products to help to get you covered.

Whether or not you already had knowledge of insurance concepts before you immigrated to Canada, you need to know insurance is part of our life while living in North America. I never bought any insurance products before moving to Canada. I came from a background in which talking about death and illness was regarded as being very unlucky. I have the mindset that bad things will not happen if we do not talk about them.

My mother, who was always very healthy, never talked about preparing for an estate plan. Then, without warning, she had a stroke during a dinner at a restaurant, and died suddenly. She had also refused to take a lump sum pension payment from her pension plan just before her death, since she thought she would get much less than taking the income for 20 more years.

There are very few things in life that are guaranteed to happen. Unfortunately, death is one of them. Until one day scientists find the solution, we have to accept the reality and make sure we have a Plan B to take care of our debt and our responsibilities to our family.

What Risk?

Some risks you have complete control over, like keeping your car well-maintained, or turning off the water or the gas stove so you won't have a flood or fire in your house. And if you sell tulips, or other goods and services, you can insure against future losses in business income. Some risks we have no control over. For example, an earthquake is nature's disaster; and being hit by a drunk driver is caused by other people's behaviour and mistakes. What if you could assess your potential risks and find a way to reduce or even transfer the risks to someone else?

Do These Sound Familiar to You?

Today, our busy lives are not only full of opportunities, but also full of risks — known and unknown. If you do not have enough resources to prepare for those losses, we still have many types of risk management products to help us to recover from the expected and unexpected hardship. Do you see yourself in any of the following scenarios?

An international traveller

You are the main income earner and you often travel on business. You are facing many risks. Not only will you or your family suffer a loss of income if the unexpected happens, they could lose you permanently. You need life, disability and critical illness insurance.

A busy mom

Maybe you are a stay-at-home mom; you take the kids to school and for after-school activities on a daily basis. The stress you have is more than others can imagine.

There are irresponsible drivers on the road, you are on a tight schedule, and you are multi-tasking all the time. If something happened to you, your spouse/partner would need to pay for someone else to take care of you and your children. Life and critical illness insurance can help pay for medical bills and provide income to help support your family.

A family history of critical illness

If you have a family history of heart or high blood pressure issues, you might have a high risk of the same illnesses as well. One out of three Canadians develops a critical illness during their lifetime. It is a scary statistic. Combine these risks together and you are at a very high risk of critical illness. Get critical insurance as early as possible. The younger you are, the better the chance you will be approved.

A person with young or elder dependants

If you have young kids or elders to take care of in your household but do not have enough savings, you face a large financial burden if you are not able to work. *"TD Economics estimates raising a child born today to the age of 18 can cost as much as $233,000..."* (CNW Nov 5, 2013) and taking care of an elder is not any less because the medical expenses could increase with aging. But this is only money lost, not life-threatening. You need disability and critical illness insurance to replace that income for a period of time in the event something goes wrong. If you pass away, then these people who depend on you will be devastated not only mentally, but financially as well. You need life insurance to cover the continued expense of caring for them, as well as the expense of children's post-secondary education.

A homeowner

Your home is beautifully refinished and located in a very desirable area, but you do not know how much coverage is in your house insurance contract. In case of fire your insurance coverage might not reflect the real market value of the cost of rebuilding the house or the value of the contents of your loss.

A car owner

You drive an expensive car and work in busy downtown. You face the risk of getting scratches on your car in a parking area, or accidents may occur because some other people are aggressive drivers. Do you have a good amount of coverage in case an automobile accident is your fault?

Single with no dependents

Compare to others, you are a free bird with less responsibility. But your close friend survived a stroke, and needs two years to recover. You start to wonder, if that happened to you, who would take care of you, since you live totally on your own. You would need to hire someone to care of you. You would need some resources to cover the caretaker expenses, on top of paying the regular bills. Critical illness, disability and long-term care insurance could help you through these life events.

A business partner

If you own a business with a partner and you do not have a buy-sell agreement, you can only wish for the best and hope nothing bad will happen. Unfortunately, business partnerships do not always go smoothly. One of the most important things you need to do before you partner with someone is to find a good lawyer and draft a buy-sell agreement. But that is not the end of the story. Do you have enough money to buy your partner out when your business relationship changes?

A business owner

If you own a business and you rely on certain others for your business, you face a high risk if something happens to these key employees. You either have to pay that person well or have a Plan B, which is to have enough money to pay for the cost of hiring or training someone else to replace this key person. Key person insurance is the solution in this situation.

A dental patient

If you have no dental or extended medical insurance, you will not die and become bankrupt from dental problems, but, you could suffer financially. Your options are to look for a job that offers this kind of employee benefit, or to get your own individual extended health coverage. If you own a small business, you are in luck. You could set up your own group plan, which is cheaper than an individual plan. Also it has potential taxation benefits.

An empty-nested parents

If your kids are all grown up and you are starting to plan for retirement, you may be wondering if living with your children when you are elderly is a good choice, if they are able and willing to offer this option. You will need to plan ahead for a few different scenarios. Long-term care insurance can offer another option for you.

Solution: Risk Control and Risk Financing

I know a family who own a big business. The three family members always drive their own cars to the same office. They also travel a lot locally and internationally on business and vacation. Again, they do not fly together. While this family appears to take a lot of risks, in fact, they have lower exposure to risk than less adventurous families. This is because they adopt a strategy called 'risk control and risk financing'. First of all, you try to avoid risk. When there is a chance something could harm your physical body, it might be a good idea to give it up for the sake of your family and yourself. If you are really not willing or you cannot give that up, then your other option is to adopt a risk reduction strategy.

For example, you should keep your car well-maintained to reduce the chance of operating problems that could lead to a breakdown or accident. Similarly, if you have a speed boat, you should follow safety precautions. Taking a driver safety course for cars or boats can reduce your insurance in both categories. The make and model of your vehicle can influence your insurance costs. I compared the annual insurance cost from different vehicles before I purchased my last car. The results were surprising. One model was $10,000 more expensive than the other one, but the annual insurance cost was much cheaper!

On the other hand, even if we do our best to avoid or reduce risks, we still cannot control mistakes made by others. No matter where the mistakes come from, in the end, we must face the potential financial loss. The Dutch tulip sellers had a better idea. The family I just mentioned here also understood it well. They have proper insurance coverage in case the risk avoidance strategy fails. The solution is to transfer or share these financial risks with others by using insurance products or social programs.

Social Programs or Insurance Products

Today, a major concern of prosperous Western economies such as Canada's is whether or not the government will be able to continue to fund retirement pension plans, health care and other social programs. A growing debate surrounds whether individuals and the private sector should play a role in financing the retirement of aging baby boomers. No matter what side of the debate you are on, it is worthwhile to ask yourself if you want to risk leaving your retirement income in the government's hands or be more proactive and do more to prepare financially for your future.

Social and assisstace programs are meant to give you very basic support. However, there are restrictions and it can be changed depending on how much funding the government can afford, since social welfare programs are supported by taxpayers. In Canada, there are different social programs. You need to know Employment Insurance (EI), and government-sponsored pension plans such as: the Canada Pension Plan (CPP), Old Age Security Program (OAS), Guaranteed Income Supplement (GIS) and the Allowance. You do not get all these benefits automatically just because you become Canadian permanent residents. Each program has its own eligibility rules.

More Canadians are reaching the age of retirement and there are fewer people in the workforce to support the social system, which is a bigger challenge than before.

In 2011, census data showed for the first time that there were more people in the age group 55 to 64 (typically the group in which people leave the labour force) than the age group 15 to 24 (typically the age group in which people enter the labour force). **The number of seniors aged 65 and over increased by 14.1% between 2006 and 2011 to nearly five million. This rate of growth was higher than that of children aged 14 and under (0.5%) and people aged 15 to 64 (5.7%)** (Census May 29, 2012 - The Canadian Population in 2011: Age and Sex).

On the other hand, if you own an individual insurance policy, you know exactly what you are getting, even if you lose your job or the government changes the rules of the social program. For example, in 2012, some changes were made to CPP and OAS, GIS and the Allowance programs. As long as you declare every fact to the insurance company on your application and go through the underwriting process before the insurance company offers you a contract, your risks are covered.

What Type of Insurance do You Need?

The market of insurance is very competitive. All the different competing offers can make choosing the right insurance coverage for you even more confusing. Increasingly, insurance companies are enticing clients with deals that range from the suspiciously attractive to the very risky. For example, you may see ads for "no medical exam required" or an insurance policy at "lowest initial cost" that may quickly increase and become expensive. These offers might imply hidden costs or even issues at claim. You can take a number of steps to ensure you choose the right Canadian insurance company and agent.

- Ensure the agent is licensed with a provincial insurance council.

- Ensure the broker belongs to a professional association such as the Insurance Association of Canada.

- Do not rely on references from friends and family alone. Each person has very different insurance needs. What they know might be limited.

- Once you have a contract, take it to your lawyer for advice if you do not understand it well.

- Read about Canadian insurance coverage beforehand so you have knowledge beyond what the agent is telling you.

The Financial Consumer Agency of Canada advises consumers not to pay a fee to an insurance broker. They are paid by the insurance companies they represent.

Mortgage Insurance vs. Individual Life Insurance

When you apply for a mortgage, all financial institutions will ask you to buy mortgage insurance if you do not have life insurance. Be very cautious of this offer.

The CBC Market Place program discussed these offers in detail on February 6, 2008 in "*In Denial—Mortgage Insurance: Not Always a Sure Thing.*" There are a few things that must be considered. To start with, when you apply for mortgage insurance, the process does not require underwriting. This means that after you die, your claim can easily be rejected because you did not go through the underwriting procedure. Not only have you wasted your entire premium, more importantly, your family finds out you do not have the coverage when they most need the money.

The second thing to consider is that the beneficiary of mortgage insurance is the financial institution itself, not your family.

Last but not least, the premium on mortgage insurance covers the mortgage's original amount, which is reduced after each repayment, but your premium remains the same. On the other hand, individual life insurance gives you the same coverage from the beginning to the end of the term. The premium for short-term life insurance might be similar to that for mortgage insurance. But it is guaranteed to go to your named beneficiary because you go through underwriting before they approve your application. You should talk to a licensed insurance professional to find a better solution.

Your Insurance Needs to Change in Different Stages of Life

Insurance plays a very important role in financial planning during different stages of your life. You could require a mix of different insurance products to meet your risk management needs.

Life insurance products cover final expenses, pay off debts and estate taxes, provide income for your family and leave a legacy. The death benefit of life insurance is tax-free. In most cases, probate costs can be avoided. The death benefit could be sent to the beneficiary within a very short period of time after the insurance company receives the required information.

Term life insurance

You can choose from 5-, 10- or 20-year term insurance. This allows you to choose insurance suitable for risks within certain periods of time, and with a purpose, such as covering a mortgage for 20 years, supporting your children for another 10 years or funding your business with a buy-sell agreement or protecting operations with key person insurance, and so forth. Once the term is up, the term life insurance policy expires. The premium will be increased every time the insurance policy renews, and often a large percentage of the premium depends on your age. Re-enforcing the stereotype of men as the household breadwinners and protectors, most term life insurance holders in Canada are men. With the trend of women contributing to a larger percentage of household income and the increase in female-led households, more women should be considering term life insurance. The number of single-parent households has doubled in Canada over last four decades to reach 16.3% in 2011. My suggestion is that even if you are not a single parent, or you are not a breadwinner in your household, you still should have life insurance. Don't you want your family to deal with less financial stress if you pass away? There is enough adjustment your family needs to make if they lose a family member.

Term to 100 life insurance

This sounds like term life insurance but it gives you permanent insurance coverage. Most insurance companies classify it as permanent insurance. The cost is cheaper than whole life and universal life insurance, but it usually has no accumulated cash value.

Permanent life insurance

This includes participating whole life and universal life insurance. You can choose to finish the total premium payments within 10, 15 or 20 years, or you could pay until you die. Both types can also allow you to build up cash values that you can access during your lifetime. Universal life insurance, for example, can provide a tax-efficient investment vehicle in addition to insurance. If you have contributed the annual maximum to a Registered Retirement Savings Plan (RRSP), or you choose not to invest in a RRSP at all, you may choose to save on a tax-free basis by placing additional funds in a universal life insurance policy. The investment in a universal life plan is tax-deferred as long as it is not withdrawn. Upon retirement, a financial planner can inform you of various strategies for using both your RRSPs and universal life insurance investments as income in a tax-efficient and potentially tax-free manner.

Disability insurance

Disability insurance products are intended to replace up to two-thirds of your before-tax earned income while you are disabled and cannot work. The individual disability insurance gives you lots of flexibility, such as non-cancellable features, different waiting periods and coverage, no matter why you are disabled. The level of disability insurance among workers is low considering the increasing number of workplace health and safety incidents. In addition to assessing disability insurance options for workers, more business owners are considering disability insurance for partners to compensate for a loss to the firm if a disability leads to losses to the company.

Critical illness insurance

Critical illness insurance usually pays you a one-time lump sum payment after you survive for 30 days from any of a list of 24 different kinds of critical illnesses. It was founded by heart surgeon Dr. Marius Barnard. In Canada, one in three Canadians in their lifetime develops a serious life-altering illness such as heart disease, cancer or stroke. Critical illness insurance offers money when you need it the most, and you can decide how to spend the money. The Income Tax Act of Canada currently has no specific provisions addressing critical Illness yet, which means the benefit is most likely treated as tax-free.

Long-term care insurance

Long-term care insurance provides a tax-free payment of $150 to $2,000 per week for you to use at home or in a facility, when you cannot perform at least two out of six daily living activities such as bathing, dressing, eating and toileting. It is a new concept to some cultures. In these cultures the seniors are taken care of by their children when they are not able to. You now have other options. Long-term care insurance provides you with the freedom to be independent and take that burden off your family. Annual nursing home fees can exceed $50,000. More people are including nursing home coverage in their long-term financial planning. Thus, it is important to be aware of when coverage begins and any exemption periods. As my mother's sudden death and many other people's unexpected illness demonstrate, sometimes you require insurance coverage earlier than when you might have planned for it.

Group insurance

For business owners, group insurance and extended health insurance (including dental care and so on) are a great way to make employees feel secure with your company in a competitive market. The group plan can be set up for a small company with as little as three people. This expense can be deducted from your business income. It is a win-win for employer and employee.

C H A P T E R 5

Building Wealth in Canada

OK, Go On...

If you are like my aunt, who links wealth only with real estate property and jewellery, you are not alone. She used to say, *"We all work for rocks: real estate properties and diamonds."* Well, she did not know that the houses in Canada are mostly built with wood. Over thousands of years of human history, people from different countries and cultures have considered being landlords as one of the symbols of being wealthy. Investing in real estate property and/or precious metals such as gold or silver was the way to build wealth. The good news is that today in Canada there are many other ways to accumulate wealth. There is no doubt that real estate should be a part of your investment portfolio. You can see it, you can touch it, and you can live in it. It offers us comfort, but we also have other opportunities to diversify our asset portfolio, and there are taxation benefits from doing so.

What is Wealth?

Wealth is simply what you have minus what you owe. Sometimes it is referred to as net worth. Someone lives in a big house or drives an expensive car and so on. It does not necessarily mean that person is wealthy, unless the market value of those properties is bigger than the loan or, better, without a loan. To put it simply, there are two ways to build wealth: you either reduce your overall debt or you increase your assets. To reduce your debt you could pay off your mortgage, car loan, credit cards and personal loans, etc. To increase your assets, you could start saving and/or investing.

With the enjoy-now-and-pay-later habit retail is promoting and the live-for-the-moment philosophy many believe in, lots of Canadians have net debt instead of net worth. I recently saw an example of this attitude while at a comedy show. The stand-up comedian, a lady in her early forties and from a famous national TV comedy show, was making fun of her experience with a financial planner. When the financial planner looked at her net worth statement and asked her, *"What will happen to you when you are 65 and no longer working, and you continue spending like this, instead of saving?"*, the pragmatic lady told the audience her strategy is to jump from a bridge and she will no longer have to worry. She does not have children so has no expense there. But saving for a down-payment still seemed to be very difficult so she never bothered. I could not laugh at that joke. I shook my head in the dark. But lots of people in the audience laughed…

We all want to increase our assets. Saving is the first step to consider. Saving simply means not spending. So the amount you save equals your income minus your expenses. Saving is a relatively passive approach to wealth accumulation. In contrast, investing is a more active approach. Investing simply means you purchase an investment with the intention of earning a return. Bear in mind the average inflation rate is at 3% per year. If you are like my grandmother, who hid her money under the bed, you are losing 3% from your capital every year. So the way to build your wealth is to invest in a combination of well-diversified assets to reduce overall risk with the goal of earning more than inflation and growing your savings more quickly.

Investments are often thought of in terms of cash, mutual funds, stocks and bonds. However, they also include other tangible assets, such as real estate, gold and silver, cars, antiques, jewellery, art, my stamp collection my mother lost, and so on. Intangible assets are property such as a copyright and/or patents.

Sources of Income

Understanding your sources of income is critically important. Your net income will be different, depending on different income sources.

For people who are working, here are some possible income sources:

1) Employment income including part-time or full-time employment.

2) Business income including rental income.

3) Investment income including non-registered investments and registered accounts such as a Tax-Free Saving Account.

4) Inheritance and/or lottery...

For people who are retired or not working, here are some possible income sources:

1) Personal savings including Registered Retirement Saving Plan (RRSP); Registered Retirement Income Fund (RRIF); Tax-Free Saving Account (RRSP) and non-registered savings.

2) Government-sponsored pension plans including Canada Pension Plan (CPP); Old Age Security (OAS); Guaranteed Income Supplement (GIS) and the Allowance.

3) Employer-sponsored pension plans, including Employer Pension Plan; Group Registered Retirement; Group RSP and Deferred Profit-sharing.

4) Home equity.

5) Selling capital properties.

6) Cash value in insurance policies.

7) Others sources such as from family trust, spousal trust, etc.

8) Lottery.

Understand How Your Income is Being Taxed in Canada

Taxes on wealth have such a large influence on personal income that sometimes people move to and from countries based on tax rates. While immigrants settle in Canada due to its stable financial climate, in other countries such as France wealthy people have left because of new tax structures. Famously, actor Gerard Depardieu rescinded his French citizenship over a 75% tax on the wealthy and has chosen to live in Russia and pay its flat tax. *"The failing economy and harsh taxes...sending thousands packing- to Britain's friendlier shores."* (Down and out: the French flee a nation in despair - Oct 20, 2013 at The Telegraph by Anne Elisabeth Moutet).

Taxes are a challenge we all face and our financial success depends, in part, on how we meet this challenge. In general, there are four ways to reduce your tax bill.
In general, there are four ways to reduce your tax bill:

1. Conversion: convert assets into tax-efficient investments

2. Deduction: use existing tax credits to reduce your overall taxable income

3. Division: income split with your spouse or children within legal restrictions to reduce your overall family unit taxable income

4. Deferral: choose investments that allow you to defer the payment of taxes.

How much tax you will pay depends on two things:
1. Your marginal tax rate

2. The type of investment income you receive.

Your marginal tax rate (MTR) = your highest federal tax rate + highest provincial tax rate.

For example, you have taxable income of $50,000 in 2013. You are in the 22% tax bracket for calculating federal taxes. You also live in Ontario which requires you to pay provincial tax of 9.15% on taxable income. In total your Marginal Tax Rate (MTR) is 31.15%. This is calculated as the federal marginal tax rate + provincial marginal tax rate, which is 22% + 9.15%. **Immigrants should be aware that each province has a different provincial income tax rate and tax credit rate. Both federal and provincial tax rates are based on graduated increases. You pay more taxes when you earn more. Also you could belong to another tax bracket with one dollar difference.**

Your investment plan needs to consider all the financial possibilities, including the impact to your annual tax bill.

Different types of income are taxed at different rates, depending on your level of income and the province of your personal residence. Understand that this can have a significant impact on your financial success.

To give you a general idea, if you have a $50,000 taxable annual income in June 30, 2013, and assume you live in Ontario with a Marginal Tax Rate of 31.15%.* This is a very rough example. The numbers are based on the basic personal tax credit and ignore the non-refundable tax credits. You need to see a tax professional for your individual case.

Your marginal tax rate on interest income/salary income is 31.15%.
Your marginal tax rate on RRSP withdrawal is 31.15%.
Your marginal tax rate on capital gains is 15.58%.*
Your marginal tax rate on eligible dividends is 13.43%.*
Your marginal tax rate on ineligible dividends is 16.65%.*

You can see clearly here what a difference different tax rates will make. Do the math yourself. If you invest your money in GICs (guaranteed investment certificate), you earn interest income, and it is 100% taxable at 29.70%. On top of this, if you lock your money away from one year to five years at a 1.5-2.3% annual interest rate right now, minus inflation of 3% - and, it is not redeemable before the end of the term! - you are actually guaranteed to lose your capital investment.

Inflation

Inflation is a silent killer. Understanding how inflation works will help you make the right investment decision, and it will help you plan for your retirement.

If we only use 3% as the annual inflation rate for the calculation, and use $1,000 as the value of an investment today, in five years it will drop to $863 of today's value; in 10 years it will drop to $744; and in 20 years it will drop to $554. In 30 years it will drop to $412 of today's value. The increase in inflation makes the cost of living more expensive, and reduces your purchasing power. Just look at how much a loaf of bread costs 10 years ago and how much it costs today.

"Don't Put All Your Eggs in One Basket" Means Something Else

The principal rule of diversification is famously stated as, *"Don't put all your eggs in one basket."* But it does not mean you should not put all your money with the same financial institution. It means you should diversify your whole investment portfolio. When you invest in asset classes, such as stocks, mutual funds, segregated funds, bonds and ETF, etc., it is very important to know what sector you are investing in. Different funds/shares offered by different banks/financial institutions/company may invest in the same sector or even the same companies. In that case, you do not achieve the goal of diversification of your investments.

Diversification

There are different ways to diversify your portfolio. Choose different assets classes; choose company shares from different industries/sectors; choose shares from companies with different sizes in different stages of growth; choose assets from different geographic areas; even choose bonds that have different maturities.

Asset Allocation

Many financial experts agree that asset allocation is one of the most important factors in determining returns on a long-term investment portfolio. It is also one of the most important decisions an investor makes. It is an investment strategy that balances risk and reward by allocating a portfolio's assets according to an individual's goals, risk tolerance and investment time horizon.

Different Asset Classes

Real estate

Some immigrants come from a culture that believes real estate is the best investment option. True, lots of wealthy people built their wealth from the real estate market. But you do need to know the Canadian real estate market well. Some areas appreciate more than others. It is not a sure thing that it will have the same growth rate as before. Should you buy real estate? Absolutely! With the principal residence exemption rule, many Canadians consider their principal residence to be their future retirement income. I consider real estate to be one important asset class. One thing to be considered is that real estate property may not always be sold as fast as you wish at the price you want. You certainly should not invest in real estate and consider that is your only emergency fund.

Taxes on real estate will depend on your use. Real estate used as a personal residence, or as rental properties, or for business purposes is all subject to different tax rates. Rental income on property owned by a non-resident is usually subject to a federal 25% withholding tax, unless a tax treaty between Canada and your home country reduces the tax rate. Perhaps you are in the process of obtaining Canadian residency. If a spouse already has residency, you may want to consider putting real estate in his/her name.

Mutual funds and segregated funds

Equities and fixed income instruments have different levels of risk and return over time, and it is impossible to accurately forecast future prices. You can stabilize your investment returns by investing in a well-balanced and diversified portfolio. Mutual funds pool shares from many companies to help you reduce the level of market risk you may experience while achieving your long-term investment goals.

As I described earlier in this chapter, capital gains are taxed at a lower rate than interest income. Only 50% of capital gains is subject to taxes. On dividend-paying investments, Canadian investors benefit from more favourable tax treatment because of the dividend tax credit. The actual tax rate varies among provinces.

If your mutual fund pays a distribution which is reinvested, it may not be taxable in the year it is received. The larger tax bill hits when the investment is sold. Interest on fixed income investments such as bonds and treasury bills are 100% subject to your Marginal Tax Rate (MTR) income tax. Therefore, it might be a good idea to keep these fixed income investments in your RRSP or TFSA Accounts.

A segregated fund is another good choice for conservative investors. What is a segregated fund? In simple words, a segregated fund is a mutual fund offered by an insurance company. It offers different guarantee options, such as maturity and death benefit guarantees. Some segregated funds also offer income stream options, acting like a paycheque while the capital is still being invested.

There are some good reasons to use segregated funds. Usually you can only name beneficiaries for your registered accounts, such as RRSP, TFSA and RRIF. You could name your beneficiary in the segregated fund contract, even if that is not a registered account. The value of the contract is paid directly to the named beneficiary upon the owner's death. This is important especially for those who value privacy. The value of the segregated fund does not form part of your estate, if the beneficiary of the segregated fund contract is not your estate. It means that it is not subject to probate fees. It also saves time going through the probate process. The potential for creditor protection is another feature that attracts business owners.

Business ownership

Don't forget a business ownership is also an asset class. Canada is a good place to start a business. In a recent survey from PWC (PriceWaterhouseCoopers), one of the largest professional service firms in the world, out of 185 countries Canada ranked an impressive eighth in terms of the 'ease of taxation' on small-to-mid-sized family businesses. Measurements included the tax rate and the number of hours it takes to comply with tax regulations.

There are many tax-saving opportunities for having a small business ownership in Canada. To name a few:

There is the potential for income splitting with your employed family members; and the potential to defer income by timing of salary and bonus payments. You also have the opportunity to set up a registered pension plan and private health care plan. Do not forget there is also the Federal limit of $500,000 as the Small Business Deduction - it can only be claimed by certain private corporations, but it gives a lower tax rate on the first $500,000 of active business income. Although the corporate tax rate varies across provinces, it is generally lower than the personal tax rate. It can be advantageous to retain earnings within a corporation. When you want to sell your business, the $750,000 lifetime capital exemption upon the disposition of a qualifying small business interest is very attractive.

Succession planning is one of the major concerns of small businesses. A financial planner can work with your accountant and help you assess tax strategies that manage taxes more efficiently across your business and personal income tax obligations.

Permanent insurance

Permanent insurance policies can do much more than just leave some money to your named beneficiary. They are legal "tax shelters" from an investment point of view. Also they are able to offer a stable income stream for the policy owner. I will discuss these options in Chapter 7.

ETF

What is an ETF? ETF is the abbreviation for exchange-traded fund, and "is an investment fund traded on stock exchanges, much like stocks." (Wikipedia)

ETFs became a trend in recent years, and I believe will continue have influence on the investment market. An ETF has the diversification within a portfolio as a mutual fund portfolio, but it trades like stocks; and it has lower management fees than most mutual funds. On the other hand, the burden is placed on the investors — you are the one responsible to choose the proper investments and manage your own portfolio. Also be aware of the fees. You will pay a $10-$20 flat fee to the broker each time you buy or sell. But if you have a monthly saving plan of $100 or $200, the management fees add up quickly. In my opinion, this is more for sophisticated and experienced investors, since you need to know what to invest and how to manage your own portfolio. Another thing you will also want to consider before you decide if ETFs are for you is the tax implications arising.

Other assets

There are other asset classes that I will not address in detail here, such as bonds, stocks, guaranteed investment certificates (GIC), gold, and so on.

By diversifying your whole investment portfolio, you are able to hedge against risk and provide better return over long term. It is like you are sitting on the financial equivalent of a chair with 4 legs — solid and stable.

* Resource is from Ernst & Young LLP

CHAPTER 6

Shortcuts to Wealth

You Have My Full Attention...

By knowing the financial planning process, you are always ahead of the others. Now is the time you have been waiting for. Let me show you some basic but important concepts. To help you start thinking about financial planning, I have approached the topics of this book in order according to the financial planning process. You might find different financial planners have different processes; but the whole idea is to plan according to your personal goals, needs and concerns, which should eventually cover all those areas.

To start with, risk management is the basis of financial planning; the foundation of your wealth. You should always have a Plan B in case something unexpected happens, and then you can go back and focus on Plan A to build a bright future. You cannot drive your new car away before you have insurance on it. The same idea applies here. **The most valuable thing in your life is yourself: protect yourself first.** If you do not have enough emergency funds, then make sure you have critical illness and/or disability insurance coverage in case you cannot work for a while. You do not need to die to get those benefits. That is why they are called 'living benefits'. Of course, you hope you will never need to claim them, but you have peace of mind if you need it. If you have family already, be responsible to them by having life insurance, and your will and Power of Attorney set up.

Meanwhile, you should look into your cash flow. You might need to restructure your debt first, in order to free up your cash flow. There is bad debt and there is good debt. When those goals are met, you should start saving for an emergency fund and major purchases. You have to start somewhere, even with small amounts as they will eventually grow into bigger amounts. If you never start saving, just like that comedian I mentioned in a previous chapter, you will never have a lump sum down-payment for your first home. If you were never taught a good saving habit when you were young, now you have to learn it the hard way. **Spend only what you NEED, not what you WANT! Spend only what you can afford, instead of spending first and worrying about payment later. Simple!** Saving requires discipline. That is one of the reasons most people need a financial planner— to help you to be disciplined, because it is hard to do it alone.

When the risk management strategy is in place, you are moving to the next step—building your net worth. This is the stage of your life at which you need to have the maximum cash flow. During this period, you should contribute to your RRSP. It will help to reduce your income tax, build up your retirement fund and defer income taxes until much later. You may also want to buy a home and save for your children's education as well.

A mortgage is typically the biggest debt many Canadians have in their lifetime. Choose your mortgage strategy carefully and you could save thousands of dollars. Ask your financial planner about a strategy that helps you to make your mortgage interest tax-deductible. Although this is a more complicated strategy that requires careful planning, that structure would allow a portion of your mortgage interest to be tax-deducted as an investment expense. It also offers flexibility for your cash flow, which is a bonus.

You also need an education plan (RESP- Registered Education Saving Plan) for your children. The Canadian government is there to help your next generation's post-secondary education by contributing a portion to your RESP. It is FREE money. Don't waste that chance.

Once you have a mortgage under your name, and have a family to raise, your budget will be tight for at least 18 years. Remember? Raising a child to 18 needs about $233,000. *"Average cost of an undergraduate degree while living away from home is expected to be $150,000 by 2031."*, according to recent TD research in November 2013. Again, you need to have a Plan B—life insurance-to cover your debt and offer funds to raise your children in case something happens to you before your children are financially independent.

When all these financial concerns are taken care of, you come to another stage of life. Now you can afford to spend more money on the lifestyle you want, as well as invest in rental property, even antiques and other collectables like art. Note that these investment vehicles will not give you a tax break.

Time Really is Money: Invest as Early as You Can

My mom opened a savings account for me after I was born, and she saved for years until she had enough money to deposit into a GIC (Guarantee Investment Certificate). The idea is great. But you can imagine how little the return was. Once or twice a year you get interest, and then you have to wait for another 6 to 12 months to get the second interest payment. If you deduct the income tax you NEED to pay on the interest income in Canada, as well as the inflation rate of 2 to 3% each year, it is guaranteed that your money will shrink. Savings become a loss in this instance.

Let me introduce compound interest to you. If you use your time wisely, the result is amazing. The following example assumes interest/return tax-free or tax deferred.

Let's look at Brad and his friend David. Brad is taken wise advice from his financial planner and he starts investing $2,400 from the age of 20 until he is 29 (for 10 years). He stops his contribution because he needs that cash for his mortgage, but his capital contribution continues to grow by itself while he is busy with life. 35 years later, by the time he turns 65, his portfolio has the potential to grow into a market value of $353,401. He contributes only $26,400.

David is not familiar with this concept at first. When he understands it, he has already turned 30. Nevertheless, he starts contributing $2,400, just like Brad, for the next 35 years. By the time he turns 65, his portfolio has the potential to grow into a market value of $338,782. He has put in a total of $86,400.

In this case, the accumulation is before tax and based on an compound rate of 6.5%,invest annually and income earned is tax-deferred. You can see clearly, **10 years of investment at a total capital of $26,400 is worth more than 35 years of investment at total capital of $86,000.That is the power of compound interest!**

The Simple Way to Come Up with $200 Saving Per Month

If you think saving $2,400 per year is very difficult to do, let me ask you: Do you pick up a cup of coffee on your way to work and a second cup after lunch? Let's say it costs you $5 each day. If you and your spouse/ partner both spend $5 on coffee for 20 days each month, that is your $200 per month investment. If you invest in a TFSA (Tax Free Savings Account) you do not need to pay tax on the growth. If you invest in an RRSP, you will get a tax break to help free up your cash flow. Every day you buy your coffee, think about the lost investment opportunity. You are drinking thousands of dollars away. Use the same method, I am sure you could cut down some of your unnecessary spending and find some saving every month.

The Best Investment is the Investment that Suits Your Risk Profile

Once I met someone at a golf tournament. As soon as he knew I was a financial planner, he stopped me in the middle of the game and asked, *"What is the best investment right now in the marketplace? Is it gold? Which company's stock? Which mutual fund...?"*

My reply was, *"That depends."*

He laughed at me, *"You don't know!"*

I smiled. *"I don't know what your risk tolerance level is. Where to invest depends on how much risk you are willing to take. And whether it is for your short-term or long-term financial goals."*

From time to time, people ask me which stock or fund is the best for them, because they heard someone else say that this fund or that stock is going up fast, and so on.

The most shocking question I have been asked was from an older gentleman who told me he could not handle a drop in the stock market. *"Could you get oil options for me? My son said it is going to go up."* I looked at his risk profile, and I said, *"I really do not recommend you use your retirement income to buy those products. They are too risky for you."* I really do not want to hear that my client has had a heart attack because he made the wrong investment decision.

My questions to my clients are always: What if the stock market goes down before it goes up? How big a loss can you handle? How much risk are you willing to take? How long is your investment time horizon? Those determine what your risk profile is and the best options for your investment. When the stock market is up, we can all handle it. I have never heard of anyone having a heart attack because the market went up 40%. We are so happy for those financial gains. But when our $200,000 investment drops to $120,000, I bet many of us will start losing sleep at night. For those who do not have enough knowledge, you probably sold it at a loss, just like I did once. Because we panic!

Dollar Cost Averaging: Invest Regularly

Although the stock market has been up on average since 1802, the market has been through many ups and downs. We all know the phrase, buy low and sell high. That is how you make a profit from stocks, mutual funds and other investments, but none of us has that crystal ball to tell us when the market prices will be low or when they will be high. The easiest and best way to invest in the real world is to invest a certain amount of money regularly, no matter what happens to the market. Do not forget, when you buy a mutual fund or stock, you buy units. You should buy more units of mutual funds or company shares when the market is down. **When the stock market is down, share prices are on sale! That is the Boxing Day deal you are looking for.**

Emotional Investing—It Can Be Very Costly

I have been asked many times what investment will guarantee a profit. My answer is always the same. I don't know which ONE particular investment will guarantee a profit for you, but I do know how you will be guaranteed to lose your investment: if you buy high and sell low because of emotion. What to invest in depends on your risk tolerance level, your investment time frame and your goal for this investment. Your financial planner will have some suggestions to fit in with your individual situation. Remember, this is all about you. The best choice for others might not be the best choice for you. Do your homework and get professional advice. Do not just jump into the trends. Take responsibility for your hard-earned money. The price you pay as an emotional investor is way too high. Those who try to get the maximum gain from the trend by switching in and out of the hot performance funds often end up taking much longer to get where they want to go, because they buy the shares at the higher price and sell as the share price drops.

Special Accounts for Canadian Residents—RRSPs, TFSAs, RESPs

There is some misunderstanding about RRSPs and TFSAs from new immigrants. What are these "accounts"? They do not exactly mean regular bank accounts. **Registered Retirement Saving Plan (RRSP), Tax Free Saving Account (TFSA) and Registered Education Saving Account (RESP) are simply programs the Canadian government put into place that encourage you to save for your future retirement or children's education and so on, on a tax-deferred or tax-free basis.**

More Reasons to Invest in RRSP

The money in an RRSP grows on a tax-deferred basis, and you also receive a tax deduction on your current income tax. You need to 'earn income' from business or employment to get the RRSP contribution limit. If only one spouse has an RRSP contribution limit, s/he could contribute to a Spousal RRSP for the spouse who does not have an RRSP limit and still get the taxation benefit.

Contributing to RRSPs can potentially achieve two goals: reducing your overall income tax, and building up a retirement saving in a tax-deferred manner. Why do people not want to contribute to RRSPs? Some might hear it can cause their Old Age Security (OAS) benefit to be clawed back, and they do not want to lose that government benefit. Some business owners have a lot of expenses to claim, and it can end up that they do not have much RRSP contribution room. Many people do not have enough cash flow, or more importantly, they do not have enough discipline to contribute.

You will pay income tax at the time you withdraw your RRSP funds, and you do need to pay back some or all of your OAS benefit if your income passes a certain threshold. That is another reason you need a financial planner to help you to plan ahead and know what income stream to withdraw first during your retirement.

Other than the few basic investments, such as guaranteed investment certificates (GICs), compound Canadian Savings Bonds and many mutual funds, there is a long list of **qualified investments you can use for your RRSP**, a few of which are:

- **Shares listed on a prescribed stock exchange in or outside Canada**

- **A mortgage secured by real property located in Canada**

- **Limited partnership units listed on a Canadian stock exchange**

- **Gold and silver bullion coins and bars, and certificates on such investments. These are used to be non-qualified RRSP investments, but are now qualified investments. For those who love to buy gold and silver, now you have more reasons to invest in RRSP.**

The most common **non-qualified RRSP investments** are: real estate; listed personal property, such as works of art and antiques; shares of many private corporations; gems and other precious stones; and commodity futures contracts.

TFSA

A Tax Free Savings Account (TFSA), first offered to Canadians in 2009, became another great way to build up your retirement savings pool. But if you want tax relief starting from the current income-earning year, RRSPs are still the best choice for most people.

A TFSA can be used for any purpose. You do not get tax deductions for your income tax, but all the growth within the account is completely tax-free. The program started in 2009 with a $5,000 limit each year per person which increased to $5,500 in 2013. In my opinion, it is best to use a TFSA for long-term or high-return investments to maximize its tax-free benefits. For example, if you put $15,000 in a TFSA as an emergency fund, basically you have to treat it as the lowest risk kind of investment, and usually you will not get much in return. So how much tax can you actually shelter? Well, if you get over a 6% compound return on long-term investments, the taxes you save could be a lot!

RESP— One of the Best Benefits the Canadian Government Offers to Canadian Residents

In today's world, many businesses compete globally. Even on a personal level, we are no longer only competing with the people locally. If you still have any doubt, just check the online talent pools and see how many talented people in the world are competing for the same job. There are many jobs where you never need to meet the worker(s) in person.

Immigrants who have grown up in countries with vast populations understand the power of education. You might hear stories about how some parents sacrifice everything for their children's education. Because they believe that in most cases, a higher education means better job opportunities in the future, and a better chance to have a greater quality of life. Therefore, many immigrants would agree with me that the RESP (Registered Education Savings Plan) is one of the best benefits currently being offered by the Canadian government.

The Canadian government understands education is essential for the country's future growth. Not only is school from kindergarten to Grade 12 truly free, the government even offers support to encourage parents to save for their children's post-secondary education. Depending on your family income, you can get 20-40% from the government to match your contribution up to an annual limit, in the form of a basic Canada Education Savings Grant (CESG) and Enhanced Canada Education Savings Grant. If your children were born in or after 2004, you might be able to get a Canadian Learning Bond (CLB) as well.

Keep in mind, RESP is a registered plan associated with your social insurance number (SIN). You can contribute to different financial institutions. From 2007, the annual RESP contribution ceiling was removed; the lifetime contribution limit was increased to $50,000.

I have only touched on the advantages and considerations of using registered accounts. To learn how to best use these investments as part of your financial planning, sit down with a financial planner and find out more details.

A Special Investment and Income Stream

Is it Safe and Will it Last?

When I considered getting permanent insurance for myself, I did my homework. I calculated the total premium for the face amount I would get, and then compared how much I would possibly get if I invested the same amount in the riskiest investment I wanted to make. As soon as I saw the numbers, the decision was easy.

Permanent Life Insurance as an Investment

Growing up with a mother who was an accountant, I learned to be a person who saved money at an early age. I also learned to spend on things that are important. A permanent insurance product gives me the peace of mind knowing that my family will be taken care of if I pass away. When I realized that permanent insurance is not only an insurance product, it can also be considered as an investment product, I thought: this couldn't be better. In fact, it might be one of the best long-term investments you can find in Canada.

Both participating whole life and universal life insurance products offer the chance for you to build a cash value and shelter the growth from income tax. You could deposit extra money other than your premium into your insurance policy. It is invested in a tax-sheltered manner. **Dwayne Daku describes the details of this strategy in his book "*15 Secrets the Taxman Doesn't Want You To Know*", and calls it is "*the GREATEST tax shelter available in Canada.*"** But if you are unable to, or do not want to, contribute more than your premium, then I can show you how to get cash value and earn tax-free growth even if you do not deposit anything extra.

How Does It Work?

Here is how it works. Participating whole life insurance has its unique structure. It combines life insurance protection with a tax-advantaged investment component. You could get dividends from the insurance company. It requires you to pay nothing other than your premium. You will ask: Why do they pay me dividends, I do not own any shares in the insurance company? These unique dividends are different from shareholders' dividends. Once these dividends are given to you, they become the cash value within your participating whole life insurance policy. That cash cannot be reduced or used without your permission, other than for paying your premium.

Historical Returns of These Dividends

Let's look at some numbers. From 1952 to 2011, the S&P composite total return index delivered 17 years of negative returns, including three years when it dropped over 20%. But there is an insurance company in Canada that never offered less than a 5.9% dividend scale interest rate. From 1982 to 2011, the average dividend scale interest rate from this company was 9.7%. During the same period, the S&P/ TSX composite total return index was 9.1%. Government of Canada 5 to 10-year bonds were 7%. The standard 30-year deviation (since 1982) of the S&P/ TSX composite total return index is 16.6; for Government of Canada 5 to 10-year bonds it was 3.1; and for this company it was 1.7.* Translation: During this period of time, the dividend scale interest rate from this life insurance product was better than the stock market and these government bonds, and fluctuated the least of the three. There is more than one insurance company in Canada offering this kind of insurance product. When you buy participating whole life insurance, ask your insurance agent for the update of dividend scale from different insurance companies. If you apply for a policy with large coverage, you might also want to compare the assets held by different insurance companies.

Example of a 50-year-old Business Owner

Here is a case of a 50-year-old business owner; male, non-smoker, quoted with a standard rating. He is at a 43.7% personal marginal tax rate and living in BC. He wants to have $2,000,000 in 20 years to cover his estate taxes and leave a legacy. Sure, he might be able to make and save $2,000,000 in 20 years, or he could just leave less for his family, or give up the idea of having a legacy. There is a fourth option. I suggested permanent insurance with a face value of $1,000,000. He will pay $35,005 premium per year for 20 years, in total $700,100 over his lifetime. The number will be different with different companies and depending on the dividend scale. The below illustration gives you an idea of the potential value that could be created from a total of $700,100 investment.

Year	Age	Total cash value*	Total death benefit*
10	60	$ 129,221	$1,127,580
20	70	$1,102,718	$1,713,295
30	80	$1,904,621	$2,515,339
40	90	$2,999,061	$3,480,071

*This illustration was made in 2012 with Canada Life software and using the 2012 dividend scale interest rate, with paid-up additions chosen, and these values include non-guaranteed values.

The cash value (dividend) he receives every year is tax-free, and the value growth within the policy is tax-free. Upon his death, his named beneficiary receives the money tax-free. This is the simplest way to transfer assets to the next generation. Although these dividends are not guaranteed and will fluctuate, so will other investments. There aren't many investments in Canada that offer a better return and tax shelter with this level of low risk! You don't need to worry every day how the stock market is performing. You leave those worries to the insurance company.

Strategy for Children—Much Better Than Giving Cash

This method also can be used for a child and can provide an additional source of funds for education, a down-payment for a first home, money for a business start-up, or even supplemental retirement income. Plus, there is coverage for the child's estate. This means this strategy not only benefits your second generation, it could also benefit your third generation far into the future. The cash value can be accessed once or several times during the child's life.

If you are like my mom, who always gave cash to her grandchildren as birthday and holiday gifts, then this is a great way for grandparents to show their love, help out their grandchildren, and even benefit great-grandchildren. This is much better than just giving cash.

The earlier you start, the lower the premium is. Some parents or grandparents would like to open a savings account after the new baby is born, and save money for the child's future. This strategy offers flexibility and stability. It offers cash value plus permanent life insurance coverage that even benefits future generations.

For example, my client wants to buy life insurance for his newborn baby girl. He doesn't want to pay too much, but still wants to build up a cash value within the policy. Here is my strategy to help him achieve this goal: Buy a policy at a face value of $100,000. He will pay $1,109 for 20 years, in total $22,180. Below is the potential cash value for this baby girl in the future.

Year	Age	Total cash value*	Total death benefit*
10	11	$ 4,015	$ 131,710
20	21	$ 31,461	$ 232,653
30	31	$ 64,127	$ 363,577
40	41	$ 121,614	$ 503,247
50	51	$ 218,831	$ 660,870
60	61	$ 379,056	$ 845,837
70	71	$ 632,444	$ 1,072,049
80	81	$ 1,006,302	$ 1,363,254
90	91	$ 1,522,416	$ 1,756,203

*The illustration was made in 2012 with Canada Life software and using the 2012 dividend scale interest rate, with paid-up additions chosen, and these values include non-guaranteed values. Insured is a 1 year old female living in BC. Standard rating.

When this girl turns 18, her father could transfer ownership of this policy to her. He could still remain as the irrevocable beneficiary, so the policy cannot be surrendered for its cash value without his consent. By signing the policy over to her before the withdrawals are made, any future tax implication would also be the daughter's responsibility. However, there is no tax implication on the transfer of the ownership itself in this particular situation. *

There is also a strategy to continue growing this cash value outside the life policy in a tax-sheltered manner, and she will continue to have the insurance coverage.

Not every adult is insurable, because of his/her health or his/her personal hobbies. Insurance companies might even refuse to insure some occupations. I have seen and heard of many cases, but almost every adult has a need for life insurance. The child could use the cash value on anything, and the historical performance shows the return is stable with conservative risk. In my opinion this strategy is a win-win.

Get the Cash Value Out and Turn it into an Income Stream

There are several ways to get the cash value out from the accumulated value in a permanent life insurance policy. The three most common ways are: to use a collateral loan from a third party lending institution; to withdraw some of the cash value of the policy—partial surrender of cash value; or to ask for a policy loan directly from the insurance company.

These are complex strategies that involve lots of taxation details. All I can do here is let you know there are options. Each case is different. You should talk to your financial planner about your individual situation, and also seek tax and legal advice from your accountant and lawyer before you make a decision.

The Bottom Line

A client of mine encouraged me to share her experience with others. She bought a policy like this in her 20s. She paid it off and forgot about it. Fifteen years later she ran into a situation in which ALL her financial resources were gone, and she desperately needed money. All of a sudden she remembered this life insurance policy, and was able to survive during the most difficult time of her life, with the cash value built up within the policy. The cash value continued to grow even after she took the cash value out.

Investing in Canada is different from other countries because each country has a different taxation system and laws. So think outside your old box. Permanent life insurance is a special product. It is a life insurance product which guarantees that any beneficiary will receive benefits when you are no longer around. This is also an investment product with proven stable return for years. You could use the cash value for yourself first before you pass it onto your beneficiary. It fits in perfectly with many immigrants' low risk tolerance level.

* Canada Life Participating Life Insurance-Historical Performance (46-6401-6/12).
  Protect Families; Protect Lives (Canada Life 46-8251-11/11)

Why do I Need a Credit Report

I Pay for Everything in Cash...

What are Credit Scores?

Had you heard about a credit score system before coming to Canada? Some of you come from a culture where credit is built up by word of mouth; it is unwritten and no score attached to it. Some people DO actually trust each other and do business without a written contract. As these immigrants have moved to Canada, they have kept their habits. They pay cash for everything they purchase, because back in their old country that was the culture. Think about it; it is not a bad thing. Buy things only when you have enough cash to pay for it; you cannot get into debt this way! This might be the solution to reduce the huge consumer debt of Canadians. *"As of Q3 2013, Canadian consumers owe $ 1,360.7 billion, compared to $1,345.5 billion in Q2 2013..."* (Canadian Consumer Credit Trends Q3 2013 by Equifax Analytical Services)

Build and Guard Your Credit

In Canada your credit score is the major measurement of your creditworthiness. Every lender always checks it before approving a loan or mortgage. Your employer might ask for it before they hire you, if you apply for a position in which you deal with other people's money. Your landlord might want to know it before renting out a beautifully finished property to you.

The CBC Marketplace headline of April 8, 2010 was shocking*: "Credit scores can hike home insurance rates—insurance companies across Canada are increasingly turning to credit scores to help assess risk and determine the cost of premiums…Marketplace put it to the test and went shopping online for home insurance… Denying permission to use the credit score resulted in a quote of $3,324, compared with just $1,009 if the box was ticked to give permission."*

Why do your credit scores matter so much? Because your credit scores report speaks a lot about your personality. It is used to determine whether you are a credible borrowing candidate or trustworthy person. When one of insurance companies responed to Marketplace why they inlcuded credit scores while quoting home insurance, *"Credit score is simply a reflection of a person's level of responsibility and behaiviour when it comes to managing their financial obligations."*No wonder people go to great lengths to protect their credit scores.

Having a good credit score does pay off. So as new immigrants to Canada, you should apply for a credit card as soon as possible; build up your credit history by using the credit card first and paying the balance in full on time. Make sure you pay your cell phone and utility bills on time as well. Sometimes lenders use those as proof of your character if you do not have a long enough credit history showing on the data of the credit bureau. Even if you have enough cash to pay for it, it is better to use your credit card first, and then pay the full amount before your payment is due. Ask your bank to direct debit at least the monthly minimum payment from your bank account, in case you cannot remember all different payment dates.

Years ago when I had just come to Canada, my bank asked me to keep a 2-year term deposit with them, in order to approve a credit card for me. Things have changed since then. Some financial institutions do not ask for that deposit any more. Do your research before you apply for a credit card. Compare the interest rate and other features. Some credit cards come with the feature of extending your manufacturer warranty; some offer travel insurance if you use their credit cards to book your tickets and hotels. Some offer points toward your credit card balance. If you want to get more than one credit card, then get one from each provider (Visa, Master and American Express), because some stores and/or some countries might only accept one kind.

What Goes Into a Credit Report?

1. Your past payment history, usually the last seven years, including credit cards, retail accounts, installment loans, financial company accounts and mortgage loans. Also all the public records and collection items, such as bankruptcies, judgments and liens.

2. The current debt you owe. This includes the amount you owe on all your accounts, such as credit cards, personal loans and mortgages. How many credit accounts you have, and with what balances.

3. The length of your credit history. In general, a longer credit history will increase your credit score. If you used a credit card for years with a good payment history, but you want to cancel it and switch to another financial institution's credit card, that is not a wise move, no matter what promotion they are offering.

4. Your recent new credit account and credit inquiries. For those who do not have a long credit history in Canada, opening many credit accounts in a short time represents a greater risk. Your credit history will show how many recent inquiries for credit have been made by financial institutions, and the length of time since the last credit inquiries were made by

lenders. This could impact your credit score in a more negative way.

5. What type of credit accounts you have. Large loans such as mortgages will have bigger impact.

The Benefit of Getting Your Credit Report and Knowing Your Credit Scores

The benefit of knowing your scores is that you know how close your credit is to the next credit rating level, and this knowledge could assist you in improving your success and reducing some of your borrowing interest rates. Credit scores are generally grouped together into six levels or brackets. Different level could mean different interest rates. There are minimum scores you are required to have to be approved by lenders. If you happen to be one or two points in the next bracket, you could easily pay more or less interest at any given time, or possibly be declined for a mortgage or loan you apply for.

There are three Canadian credit bureaus: **Equifax, TransUnion and the Northern Credit Bureaus.** You can get a free credit report from either Equifax or TransUnion. Order your credit report ONLY from the official websites of the credit bureaus. Checking your credit score report regularly is highly recommended. It can help you to spot any issue at an early stage. Both credit bureaus offer credit monitoring and ID theft protection services for a monthly fee. I encourage you go to their websites to get more up-to-date information and compare service features. You will learn lots of information on their website, such as ordering the free credit file, and how to correct if there are mistakes in your credit report.

How to Protect my Investment and Identity

We have discussed many subjects in this book. Last but not least, we cannot forget one very important subject—how to protect your investment and your identity.

From time to time, you hear terrible stories about immigrants who trusted the wrong people to handle their investments. Even after those thieves disappeared with the victims' life savings, the naïve immigrants still did not dare to come forward and report it. You do not need to be afraid. It is Canada. There are ways you can protect yourself. Be responsible to yourself by educating yourself with knowledge and putting it into action.

A Few Things You Should Know Before You Invest in Canada

Before you invest your life savings with anyone, ask if their company is a member of CDIC and CIPF. You might want to educate yourself on how much coverage this organization provides for your investment before you deposit your cheques.

CDIC (Canadian Deposit Insurance Corporation) insures deposits in banks, trust companies and loan companies against loss in case of member failure.

CIPF (Canadian Investor Protection Fund) is a not-for-profit organization that provides investor protection for investment dealer bankruptcy.

You can find out your potential financial planner/ advisor/ firm if they are registered with the following organization(s), and at good standard before you hire them:

MFDA (The Mutual Fund Dealers Association of Canada), the Provincial Insurance Council (every province has its own), and/or IIROC (Investment Industry Regulatory Organization of Canada).

Financial Consumer Agency of Canada offers lot of information for consumer to educate themselves on subjects such as protecting yourself from investment fraud and how to choose a financial planner/ advisor/ firm, etc.

Identity Theft and Identity Fraud

Identity theft and fraud are two of the fastest growing crimes in Canada today. On the RCMP's website, it describes identity fraud as, *"The actual deceptive use of the identity information of another person (living or dead) in connection with various frauds (including, for example, personating another person and the misuse of debit card or credit card data)."**

According to statistics from the Canadian Anti-Fraud Center, from January 1, 2012 to June 30, 2012, there were already 2,607 complaints about ID theft and 8,859 on ID fraud, and the ID fraud dollar loss had reached $7,556,939.* Victims of identity theft or fraud can suffer financial loss and find it difficult to obtain credit or restore it to good standing. It can have a huge impact like damaging your credit record and you cannot get approve for a loan or mortgage. The worst case is your identity is used for criminal activities without you knowing. The process of fixing the damage from identity theft and identity fraud is not easy.

Ask around, you will hear all kinds of horror stories from people you know who have been victims of ID theft and fraud. Stories such as the man who found out when he applied for a mortgage that his name and ID had been used to open an account with a cell phone company, and the debt was under his name. Thankfully the amount was not large and his credit record was not damaged yet. Another lady was not as lucky as him. Her credit card was stolen, and it was used to the maximum limit before she found out it was lost! She spent months dealing with this issue, her credit record was damaged and she was declined for an RRSP loan, which is not even a big amount. My assistant once received a phone call from a 'client' and asked to have her direct deposit account changed. I sensed something was wrong and I stopped the process. My client's information was stolen and the ID thief thought of every details to fool us: the person who called my new assistant pretended she was an elder lady and even stammered just like my client.

What Are the Identity Thieves Looking For?

It could be your full name, full address, your email address, signature, date of birth, passport number, driver's license number, social insurance number, mother's maiden name, your username and password for all kinds of online services. Credit card information includes numbers, expiry dates and the last three digits printed next to the signature panel. It could even be the place you were born, your taxation information, your phone numbers, your family information, and so on. With this information, identity thieves can easily do online and telephone shopping, etc.

How to Protect Yourself from Identity Theft and Fraud

Be careful about the information you give out. We are often asked for our email addresses, postal codes and shopping habits online, and while these can seem like innocent questions, they are often used to create a profile of you for marketing purposes. If this information gets into the wrong hands, all of that information about what you like and how you shop can provide clues that are helpful in stealing your identity. I never give my real postal codes to the retail store when the cashier asks me.

It is recommended to set up different email addresses for different purposes: one for junk mail and marketing material, one for business use and one for friends. Change your passwords regularly and never let anyone know.

You should never bring your social insurance card with you; memorize the number instead. You should not need to give away that information unless it is related to income tax. Shred all personal information before you dump it in the garbage bin. Keep your personal information secure if you are having something done at your home and always ask for the person's work ID. Check your credit card statement carefully after you receive it, if you have not enrolled in a credit monitoring plan. If you choose not to receive paper statements, then set a reminder for yourself to check after the statement date. You usually have 30 days from the statement date to dispute any errors.

I strongly suggest you take some times to visit the websites at next page **Websites of Resources and References** for more information. You can find many tips on the RCMP, Canadian Anti-Fraud Center websites, as well as the Credit bureaus websites on identity theft and fraud, and understand what to do in case you become a victim of ID theft or fraud.

* RCMP website
  The Canadian Anti-Fraud Center Monthly Summary Report July 2012

Enjoy your brand new life in this beautiful land!

Cheers!

Jessica Danli Pang

Dec 2013

http://wealthyimmigrants.com/
Email: jessica@wealthyimmigrants.com
Connect with me on LinkedIn
https://www.linkedin.com/in/jessicadanlipang

Join my group 'Chinese Investors in Canada Network' at LinkedIn and 'The Lower Mainland Power Within Group' at Meetup

Websites of References and Resource

Citizenship and Immigration Canada
http://www.cic.gc.ca/english/residents/new_immigrants.asp

Statistics Canada
http://www.statcan.gc.ca/start-debut-eng.html

Canada census 2011
http://www12.statcan.gc.ca/census-recensement/index-eng.cfm

Canada Revenue Agency
http://www.cra-arc.gc.ca/menu-eng.html

Equifax Canada
http://www.consumer.equifax.ca/home/en_ca

TransUnion Canada
https://www.transunion.ca/

Canadian Deposit Insurance Corporation (CDIC)
http://www.cdic.ca/home/Pages/default.aspx

Canadian Investors Protection Fund (CIPF)
http://www.cipf.ca/HomePage.aspx

The Mutual Fund Dealers Association of Canada (MFDA)
http://mfda.ca/about/aboutMFDA.html

Investment Industry Regulatory Organization of Canada
(IIROC)
http://www.iiroc.ca/Pages/default.aspx

Financial Consumer Agency of Canada
http://www.fcac-acfc.gc.ca/Eng/forConsumers/topics/
savings/Pages/Workingw-Travaill.aspx

Royal Canadian Mounted Police
http://www.rcmp-grc.gc.ca/scams-fraudes/id-theft-vol-
eng.htm

PricewaterhouseCoopers (PWC)
http://www.pwc.com/

Ernst & Young
http://www.ey.com/CA/en/Home

The Canadian Anti-Fraud Center
http://www.antifraudcentre-centreantifraude.ca/
english/recognizeit_identitythe.html

Recommended Reading Materials

Any book, article, audio and workshop materials
By Anthony Robbins

Excuse Me, Your Life is Waiting
By Lynn Grabhorn

15 Secrets the Taxman Doesn't Want you to Know
By Dwayne Daku

The Wealthy Barber
By David Chilton

The Millionaire Next Door
By Thomas J. Stanley, Ph.D. & William D. Danko, Ph.D.

The Millionaire Women Next Door
By Thomas J. Stanley, Ph.D.

Money Sense Magazine

The New Earth
By Eckhart Tolle

www.ingramcontent.com/pod-product-compliance
Lightning Source LLC
Chambersburg PA
CBHW020209200326
41521CB00005BA/302